EVERYDAY MATERIALS
WOOD

by
Harriet Brundle

THE SECRET BOOK COMPANY

©2020
The Secret Book Company
King's Lynn
Norfolk PE30 4LS

ISBN: 978-1-78998-079-0

All rights reserved
Printed in Malaysia

Written by:
Harriet Brundle

Edited by:
Gemma McMullen

Designed by:
Drue Rintoul

A catalogue record for this book is available from the British Library.

All facts, statistics, web addresses and URLs in this book were verified as valid and accurate at time of writing. No responsibility for any changes to external websites or references can be accepted by either the author or publisher.

CONTENTS

Page 4   What Is a Material?
Page 6   What Is Wood?
Page 8   Properties of Wood
Page 10 What Is Wood Used For?
Page 12 Wood in Water
Page 14 Wood in Heat
Page 16 Making Paper
Page 18 Musical Instruments
Page 20 Recycling Wood
Page 22 Fun Facts
Page 23 Glossary
Page 24 Index

Words that look like this can be found in the glossary on page 23.

WHAT IS A MATERIAL?

Materials are what things are made of. Some materials are natural and some are human-made.

Wood

Glass

Plastic

Metal

Every material has its own properties. A material might be very soft. This would be one of its properties.

Pyjamas, cuddly toys and pillows are all soft.

WHAT IS WOOD?

Wood comes from trees. It is a natural material. Wood can be used to make lots of different things.

Branches

Trunk

TRY THIS!
Look out of a window. How many trees can you see?

We get wood from the trunks and branches of trees.

Special tree farms grow lots of trees for us to use.

Did you know?
The number of rings inside a trunk tells you how old the tree is.

PROPERTIES OF WOOD

Some wood is very hard. It is strong and not bendy. Bark on the outside of tree trunks often feels rough and bumpy.

BE CAREFUL!
....
If you touch rough wood, you may get a splinter!

Some types of wood products are very soft. They are light and bendy. They feel smooth to touch.

Balsa wood is used to make light objects, such as model aeroplanes.

WHAT IS WOOD USED FOR?

Wood has hundreds of different uses. Hard wood can be used to make tables, chairs and even houses!

Cardboard and paper are products made from wood. They are soft and easily bent or torn.

Can you think of any other things that are made from wood?

WOOD IN WATER

When wood gets wet, sometimes it goes rotten. The water makes the wood soft and easily broken.

When living trees get wet, they don't go rotten. They need water to live and grow.

Wood can be sprayed or painted to protect it from water. When the wood has been treated it will not go rotten.

WOOD IN HEAT

Wood that is dry can be burnt by fire. Kindling is a type of wood that is used to start a fire because it burns easily.

Fire

Kindling

14

When wood is burning, the fire gives us light and heat. Once the wood has been burnt, it becomes ash.

Burning wood

Ash

Fire can be very dangerous. Be careful not to get too close!

MAKING PAPER

When trees are cut down, their wood can be used to make paper. The wood is turned into a pulp by a machine.

The machine squashes the pulp to make it flat. When the pulp is thin and dry, it is cut up to make paper.

MUSICAL INSTRUMENTS

Some musical instruments are made from wood. Pieces of wood are cut into the right shape and glued together to make the instrument.

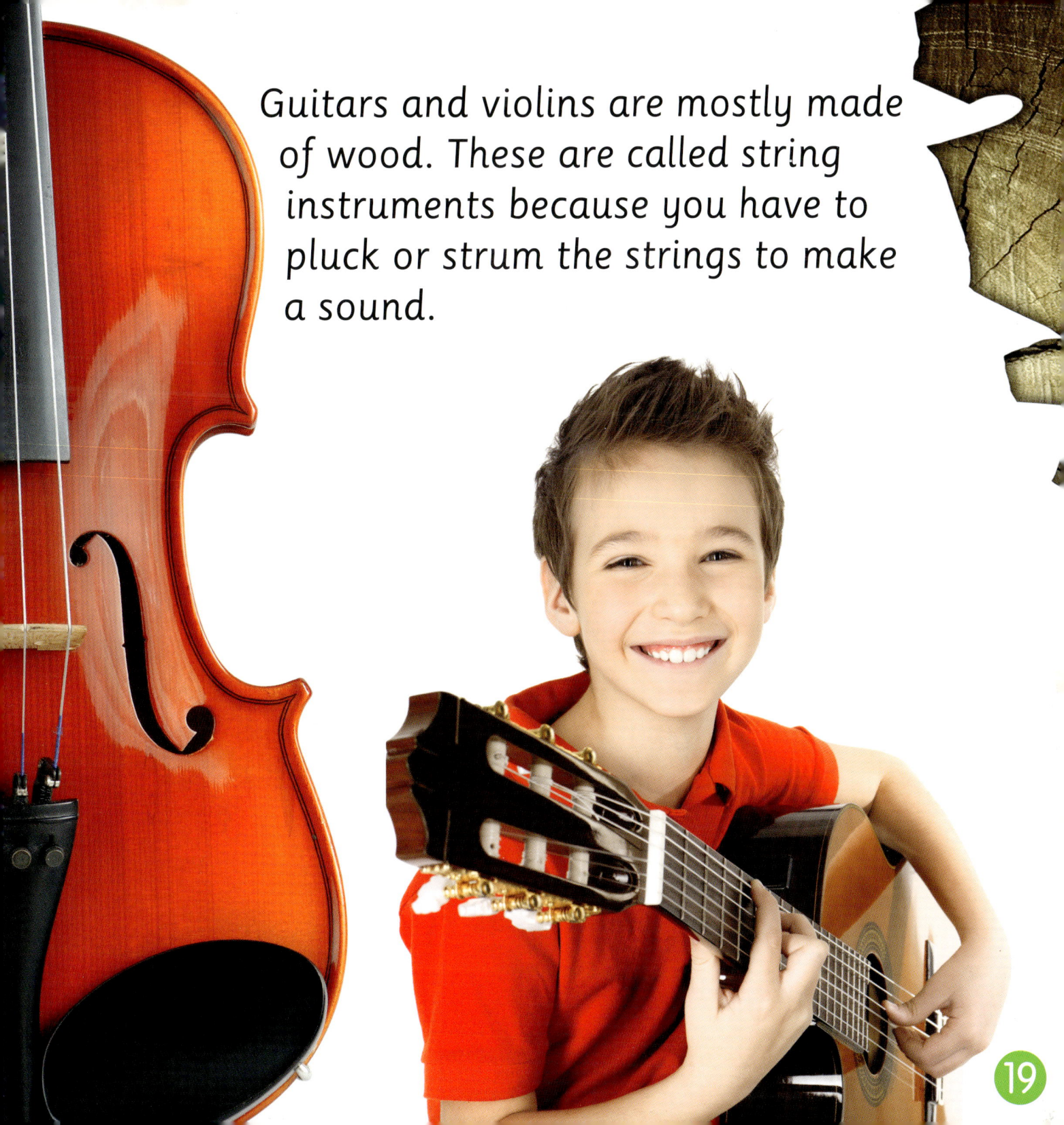

Guitars and violins are mostly made of wood. These are called string instruments because you have to pluck or strum the strings to make a sound.

RECYCLING WOOD

Wood can be recycled, which means that we can use it again. We recycle wood so that fewer trees need to be cut down.

Recycling helps to care for our planet.

Paper can be recycled. Used paper is taken to factories and washed with special soap. When it is dry it can be used again!

This symbol means that a material can be recycled.

21

FUN FACTS

Did you know that pencils are made of wood?

Some trees are more than 2,000 years old!

Experiment

Fill up a sink with water. Collect up any objects you can see that are made from wood and drop them into the water. Do they sink or float? Write down which objects sink and which objects float.

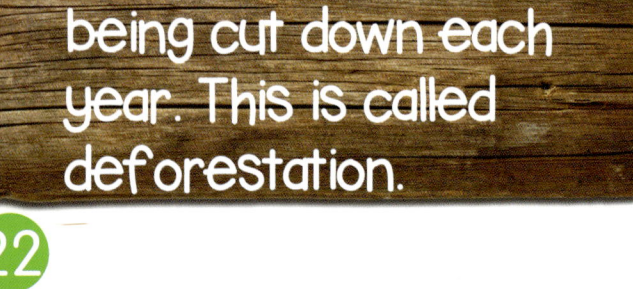

Many trees are being cut down each year. This is called deforestation.

GLOSSARY

ash
what is left after something has been burnt

human-made
something that is made by humans

natural
something that has been made by nature

properties
the different qualities of a material

pulp
a soft material, usually wet

splinter
a small, sharp piece of wood that enters the skin

treated
when a liquid is used to protect a material from something

INDEX

hard 8, 10

kindling 14

material 4–6, 21

paper 11, 16–17, 21

recycle 20–21

soft 5, 9, 11–12

trees 6–8, 16, 20, 22

Photocredits: Abbreviations: l-left, r-right, b-bottom, t-top, c-centre, m-middle. All images are courtesy of Shutterstock.com. With thanks to Getty Images, Thinkstock Photo and iStockphoto.

Front cover - Picsfive, Front cover bl, 7tl - BortN66. Front cover bm, 15l, - Calek. Front cover br - vovan. 2 - 2nix Studio. 3 - luckypic. 4 - Sunny studio. 4bl - 3445128471. 4bm - Temych. 4br - Pressmaster. 5l - wavebreakmedia. 5r - hartphotography. 6m - Zerbor. 6inset - Donjiy. 7br - SeDmi. 8 - Purino. 9 - Thorsten Schmitt. 10l - Olesya Feketa. 10m - raysay. 10r - daizuoxin. 11r - Odua Images. 11inset - Robyn Mackenzie. 12tl - C.K.Ma. 12bl - John P. Ashmore. 12br - Background Land. 13 - Dejan Ristovski. 14 - seeyou. 14inset - Laborant. 15br - Sergio Foto. 16br - LI CHAOSHU. 16tl - hauhu. 17 - hxdyl. 17inset - wavebreakmedia. 18 - Giuseppe Costantino. 19l - Getman. 19br - Valua Vitaly. 20 - Matic Stojs. 21t - Elnur. 21b - tanatat. 22l - Perutskyi Petro. 24 - SeDmi.